Richard Redhead

The Canticles from the Book of Common Prayer

pointed as they are to be sung in churches and adapted to the ancient

Psalm-chants

Richard Redhead

The Canticles from the Book of Common Prayer
pointed as they are to be sung in churches and adapted to the ancient Psalm-chants

ISBN/EAN: 9783337101336

Printed in Europe, USA, Canada, Australia, Japan

Cover: Foto ©Lupo / pixelio.de

More available books at **www.hansebooks.com**

FROM

The Book of Common Prayer,

POINTED AS THEY ARE TO BE SUNG IN CHURCHES

AND ADAPTED TO THE

Ancient Psalm-Chants,

WITH AN ACCOMPANIMENT FOR THE ORGAN,

BY

RICHARD REDHEAD.

———◆———

LONDON:

METZLER & CO., GREAT MARLBOROUGH STREET,

AND

JOSEPH MASTERS & SON, NEW BOND STREET.

1865.

NOTE.

THE fpecial objeᴄt of the prefent publication, is, to furnifh, for the ufe of the Church, an arrangement of the Canticles adapted to a greater variety of "Tones" than is generally met with, as well as the fetting forth of feveral forms of the Ancient Pfalm-Chant, as yet but little known in the Englifh Church. An harmonized arrangement of the "Magnificat," and "Nunc Dimittis," in Service-form, is alfo given.

The fyftem of pointing that has been adopted in this Book of Canticles, is the fame as that ufed by the Editor in his edition of the "Book of Common Prayer with Ritual Song." It may be defirable, however, to direᴄt attention to the main principles, viz., that words printed in italics have two or more notes fung to them; and that two words coupled together are to be fung to one note, the *latter* fyllable being the *accented one.* The firft fyllable in the "Gloria Patri," when the Intonations are ufed, is to be fung to the reciting note alfo, thus—

Glo - - - - - - ry, &c.

Contents.

AT MORNING PRAYER.

AT EVENING PRAYER.

VENITE, EXULTEMUS DOMINO.

PSALM XCV.

At Morning Prayer.

VENITE, EXULTEMUS DOMINO.

PSALM XCV.

O ‖ COME, let us fing unto the | Lord : let us heartily rejoice in the Strength of | our fal-va-tion.

2 Let us come before His prefence with thankf- | giv-ing : and fhew ourfelves glad in | Him with *Pfalms.*

3 For the Lord is a great | God : and a great | King a͡bove all gods.

4 In His hand are all the corners of the | earth : and the ftrength of the hills is | *His* al-fo.

5 The fea is His, and He | made it : and His hands pre- | par-ed the͡dry land.

6 O come, let us worfhip, and fall | down : and kneel before the | Lord our Ma-ker.

7 For He is the Lord our | God : and we are the people of His pafture, and the | fheep of His hand.

8 To-day if ye will hear His voice, harden not your | hearts : as in the provocation, and as in the day of temptation | in the Wil-dernefs ;

9 When your fathers | tèmpt-ed͡Me : proved Me, and | faw My *works.*

10 Forty years long was I grieved with this genera-tion, and | faid : It is a people that do err in their hearts, for they have not | known My *ways.*

11 Unto whom I fwear in My | wrath : that they fhould not enter | ìnto My *reft.*

Glory be to the Father, and to the | Son : and | to the Ho-ly͡Ghost ;

As it was in the beginning, is now, and ever | shall be : world without | *end.* A-men.

VENITE, EXULTEMUS DOMINO.

VENITE, EXULTEMUS DOMINO.

PSALM XCV.

O ‖ COME, let us fing | un-to the‿LORD : let us heartily rejoice in the Strèngth of | our fal-*va*-tion.

2 Let us come before His prèfence | with thankf-giv-ing : and fhew ourfelves | glad in Him with Pfalms.

3 For the LÒRD is a | *great GOD* : and a great | King a-bove all gods.

4 In His hand are all the còrners | of the *earth* : and the ftrength of the hills is | *His al*-fo.

5 The fea is His, | and He made it : and His hands pre- | par-ed the‿*dry* land.

6 O come, let us wòrfhip, | and fall *down* : and kneel before the | LORD our *Ma*-ker.

7 For Hè is the | LORD our *GOD* : and we are the people of His pafture, and the | *fheep* of His hand.

8 To-day if ye will hear His voice, hàrden | not your *hearts* : as in the provocation, and as in the day ot temptation | in the Wil-der-nefs ;

9 Whèn your | fa-thers tèmpt-ed‿Me : proved | Me, and faw My works.

10 Forty years long was I grieved with this gene- | ra-tion, and‿*faid* : It is a people that do err in their hearts, for they | have not known My ways.

11 Unto whom I fware | in My *wrath* : that they fhould not | en-ter into My reft.

GLORY BE TO THE FATHER, | AND TO THE‿SON : AND | TO THE HO-LY GHOST ;

As IT WAS IN THE BEGINNING, IS NÒW, AND | EV-ER SHALL BE : WÒRLD WITHOUT | *END.* *A*-MEN.

VENITE, EXULTEMUS DOMINO.

PSALM XCV.

VENITE, EXULTEMUS DOMINO.

PSALM XCV.

O ‖ COME, let us fing | un-to the⌒Lord : let us heartily rejoice in the Strength of | our fal-va-tion.

2 Let us come before His prefence | with thankf-giv-ing : and fhew ourfelves glad in | Him with *Pfalms*.

3 For the Lord is a | *great* God : and a great | King a⌒bove all gods.

4 In His hand are all the corners | of the earth : and the ftrength of the hills is | *His* al-fo.

5 The fea is His, | and He made it : and His hands pre- | pàred the dry land.

6 O come, let us worfhip, | and fall down : and kneel before the | Lord our Ma-ker.

7 For He is the | Lord our God : and we are the people of His pafture, and the | fheep of His hand.

8 To-day if ye will hear His voice, harden | not your hearts : as in the provocation, and as in the day of temptation | in the Wil-dernefs ;

9 When your | fa-thers tempt-ed⌒Me : proved Me, and | faw My *works*.

10 Forty years long was I grieved with this gene- | ra-tion, and⌒faid : It is a people that do err in their hearts, for they have not | known My *ways*.

11 Unto whom I fware | in My wrath : that they fhould not enter | ìnto My *reft*.

Glory be to the Father, | and to the⌒Son : and | to the Ho-ly⌒Ghost ;

As it was in the beginning, is now, and | ev-er shall be : world without | *end*. A-men.

PROPER ANTHEM FOR EASTER-DAY.

TO BE SUNG INSTEAD OF THE "VENITE."

I.   *8th Tone.*

II,   *8th Tone.*

III.   *8th Tone.*

IV.   *6th Tone.*

PROPER ANTHEM FOR EASTER-DAY.

CHRIST our || Paſſover is ſacri- | fi-ced for us : therefore | let us keep the⌢feaſt ;

2 Not with the old leaven, nor with the leaven of malice | *and* wick-edneſs : but with the unleavened bread of ſin- | ce-ri-ty and⌢truth.

3 CHRIST being raiſed from the dead, | dìeth no more : death hath no more do- | min-ion o-ver⌢Him.

4 For in that He died, He died | ùnto ſin once : but in that He liveth, He | liv-eth un-to⌢GOD.

5 Likewiſe reckon ye alſo yourſelves to be dead indeed | un-to ſin : but alive unto GOD through | JE-SUS CHRIST our⌢LORD.

6 CHRIST is riſen | from the dead : and become the firſt- | fruits of them that⌢ſlept.

7 For ſince by | man came death : by Man came alſo the reſur- | rec-tion of the⌢dead.

8 For as in | Adam all die : even ſo in CHRIST ſhall | all be made alive.   .

GLORY BE TO THE FATHER, | AND TO THE⌢SON : AND | TO THE HO-LY⌢GHOST ;

AS IT WAS IN THE BEGINNING, IS NOW, AND | EV-ER SHALL BE : WORLD WITHOUT | *END.* A-MEN.

✠

TE DEUM LAUDAMUS.

I.   2nd Tone.

II.   3rd Tone.

TE DEUM LAUDAMUS.

WE || praiſe Thee, O | God : we acknowledge Thee to | be the Lord.

2 All the earth doth worſhip | Thee : the Father ever- | laſt-ing.

3 To Thee all Angels cry a- | loud : the Heavens, and all the | Powers there-in.

4 To Thee Cherubin, and | Sè-raphin : continual- | ly do cry,

5 Holy, Holy, | Ho-ly : Lord God of | Sa-ba-oth ;

6 Heaven and Earth are full of the | Mà-jesty : of Thy | Glo-ry.

7 The glorious company of the A- | poſ-tles : *praiſe* Thee.

8 The goodly fellowſhip of the | Pro-phets : *praiſe* Thee.

9 The noble army of | Mar-tyrs : *praiſe* Thee.

10 The Holy Church throughout all the | world : doth ac- | know-ledge Thee ;

11 The | FA-THER : of an infinite | Ma-jes-ty;

12 Thine honourable, | true : and | on-ly SON;

13 Alfo the HOLY | GHOST : the | Com-for-ter.

14 Thou art the King of | Glo-ry : O | .. CHRIST.

15 Thou art the everlaſting | SON : of the | FA-THER.

16 When Thou tookeſt upon Thee to deliver | man :
Thou didſt not abhor the | Vir-gin's womb.

17 When Thou hadſt overcome the ſharpnefs of |
death : Thou didſt open the Kingdom of Heaven to all
be- | *liev*-ers.

18 Thou ſitteſt at the right hand of | GOD : in the
Glory of the | FA-THER.

19 We believe that Thou ſhalt | come : to | be our
Judge.

20 We therefore pray Thee, help Thy | fer-vants :
whom Thou haſt redeemed with Thy | pre-cious blood.

21 Make them to be numbered with Thy | Saints :
in glory ever- | *laſt*-ing.

22 O LORD, fave Thy | peo-ple : and blefs Thine |
he-ri-tage.

23 Govern | them : and lift them up for | *ev*-er.

24 Day by | day : we | màgni-fy Thee.

25 And we worſhip Thy | Name : ever wòrld with- |
out end.

26 Vouchfafe, O | LORD : to keep us this day with- |
out fin.

27 O LORD, have mercy up- | on us : have mercy
up- | *on* us.

28 O LORD, let Thy mercy lighten up- | on us : as our
truſt | is in Thee.

29 O LORD, in Thee have I | truſt-ed : let me never
be con- | *found*-ed.

TE DEUM LAUDAMUS.

III. *8th Tone.*

IV. *8th Tone.*

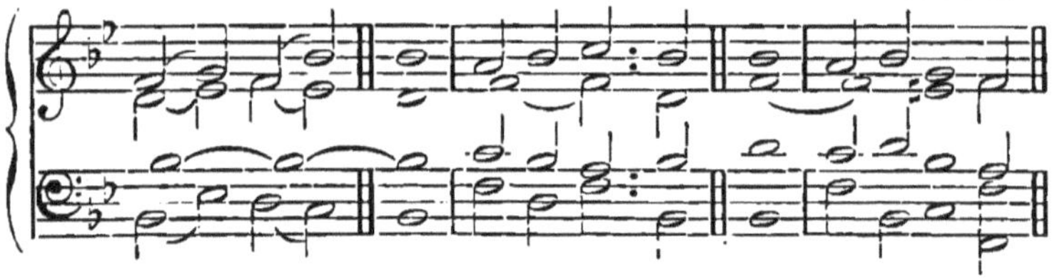

V. *8th Tone.*

VI. *5th Tone.*

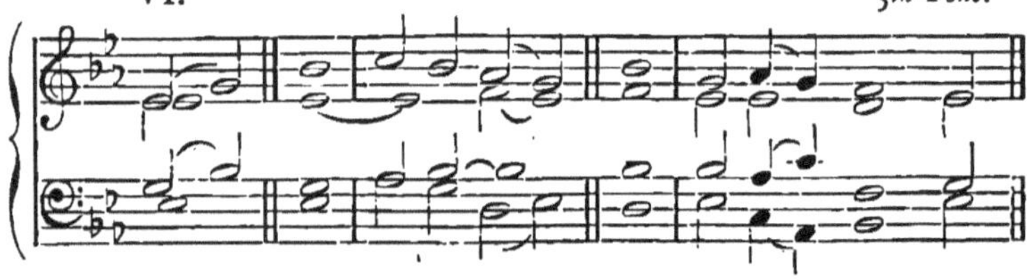

VII. *6th Tone.*

TE DEUM LAUDAMUS.

WE || praife | Thee O GOD : we acknowledge | Thee to bè the⁀LORD.

2 All the earth doth | wor-fhip Thee : the FATHER | ev-er-laft-ing.

3 To Thee all Angels | cry a-loud : the Heavens, and | all the Pòwers therein.

4 To Thee Cherubin, and | Se-ra-phin : con- | tin-ual-ly do⁀cry,

5 HOLY, | HO-LY, HO-LY : LORD | GOD OF SÀ-BAOTH;

6 HEAVEN AND EARTH ARE FULL | OF THE MÀ-JESTY : OF | . THY GLO-RY.

7 The glorious company | of the⁀A-pof-tles : praife | . Thee.

8 The goodly fellowfhip | of the Pro-phets : praife | .. Thee.

9 The noble | ar-my of⁀Mar-tyrs : praife | . . *Thee.*

10 The Holy Church throughout | all the world : doth ac- | know-ledge *Thee;*

11 The | F*A*-THER : of an | ìnfi-nite Mà-jesfty;

12 Thine honour- | a-ble, true : and | on-ly *SON;*

13 Alfo the | HO-LY GHOST : the | Com-for-*ter.*

14 Thou art the | King of Glo-ry : O | . . *CHRIST.*

15 Thou art the ever- | laft-ing SON : of | . the FA-THER

16 When Thou tookeſt upon Thee to de- | li-ver man : Thou didſt not abhor the | Vir-gin's *womb.*

17 When Thou hadſt overcome the | ſharp-nefs of death : Thou didſt open the Kingdom of Heaven to | all be-liev-ers.

18 Thou fitteſt at the right | hand of GOD : in the Glory | of the FA-THER.

19 We believe that | Thou ſhalt come : to | be our *Judge.*

20 We therefore pray Thee, | help Thy ſer-vants : whom Thou haſt redeemed | with Thy prè-ciousˆblood.

21 Make them to be numbered | with Thy Saints : in glory | ev-er-laſt-ing.

22 O LORD, | fave Thy peo-ple : and | bleſs Thine hè-ritage.

23 Go- | . vern them : and lift them | up for ev-er.

24 Day | . by day : we | mag-ni-fy Thee.

25 And we | wòrſhip Thy Name : ever | wòrldˆwith-out *end.*

26 Vouch- | ſafe, O LORD : to keep us this | dày with-out *ſin.*

27 O LORD, have | mer-cyˆup-on us : have | mer-cyˆ up-on us.

28 O LORD, let Thy mercy | light-en upˆon us : as our truſt | is in *Thee.*

29 O LORD, in Thee | have I truſt-ed : let me never | be con-found-ed.

✠

TE DEUM LAUDAMUS.

IX.

Allegro.

WE praife | Thee, O GOD : we acknowledge | Thee
to be the LORD.

2 All the earth doth | wor-fhip *Thee* : the | FA-THER
ev-er-laft-ing.

3 To Thee all Angels | cry a-*loud* : the Heavens, and |
all the Powers there-*in.*

4 To Thee Chèru-| bin, and Sè-raphin : con-| tin-ual-ly
do *cry,*

Slower.

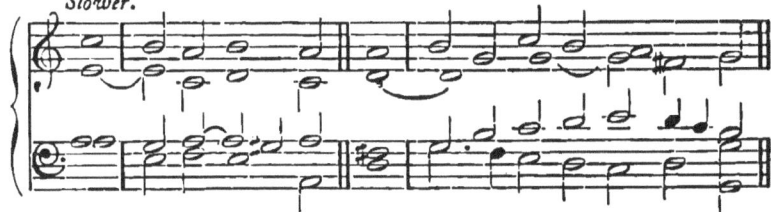

5 HOLY, | HO-LY, HO-LY : LORD | GOD OF SÀ-BAOTH ;

6 HEAVEN AND EARTH ARE FULL | OF THE MÀ-JESTY :
OF | . . *THY* GLO-RY.

Allegro.

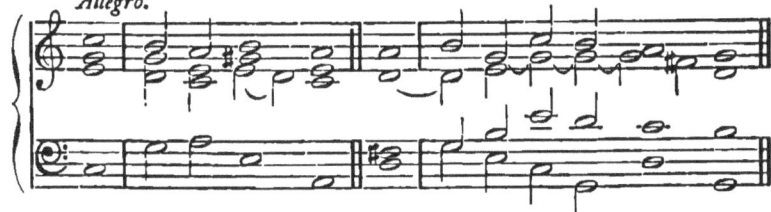

7 The glorious company | of the⌒A-pof-tles : praife | . . . .
Thee.

8 The goodly fellowſhip|of the Pro-phets : praiſe|. . . .
Thee.

9 The noble | àrmy of Mar-tyrs : praiſe | . . . . *Thee.*

10 The Holy Church throughout | all the *world* :
doth | . ac-know-lcdge *Thee;*

11 The | . . Fᴀ-ᴛʜᴇʀ : of | . an ìn-finite Mà-jeſty;

12 Thine honour- | a-ble, *true* : and | *on-ly* Sᴏɴ;

13 Alſo the | Hᴏ-ʟʏ Gʜᴏsᴛ : the | . . . . Còm-forter.

14 Thou art the | King of Glo-ry : O | . . . . Cʜʀɪsᴛ.

15 Thou art the ever- | laſt-ing Sᴏɴ : of | . . . . the
Fᴀ-ᴛʜᴇʀ.

16 When Thou tookeſt upon Thee to de- | li-ver *man* :
Thou didſt not ab- | hor the Vir-gin's *womb.*

17 When Thou hadſt overcome the | ſhàrpneſs of
death : Thou didſt open the Kingdom of | Heaven to all
be-liev-ers.

18 Thou ſitteſt at the right | hand of Gᴏᴅ : in the |
Glo-ry of the Fᴀ-ᴛʜᴇʀ.

19 We believe that | Thou ſhalt *come* : to | *bc our*
Judge.

20 We therefore pray Thee, | help Thy fer-vants : whom Thou haft redeemed | with Thy pre-cious *blood.*

21 Make them to be numbered | with Thy *Saints* : in | glo-ry ev-er-laft-ing.

22 O LORD, | fave Thy peo-ple : and | *blefs Thine* hè-ritage.

23 Go- |. vern *them* : and | lift them up for ev-er.

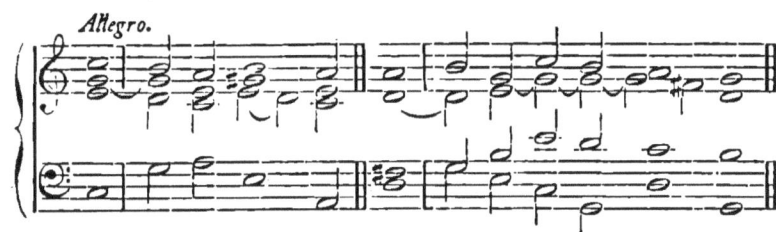

24 Day |. by *day* : we | mag-ni-*fy* Thee;

25 And we | wòrfhip Thy *Name* : ever | world with-*out end.*

26 Vouch- | fafe, O *LORD* : to keep us this | day with-*out fin.*

27 O LORD, have | mer-cy up-on us : have | *mer*-cy up-on us.

28 O LORD, let Thy mercy | light-en up-on us : as our | truft is *in Thee.*

29 O LORD, in Thee | have I truft-ed : let me | ne-ver be con-found-ed.

BENEDICITE, OMNIA OPERA.

VI.   *5th Tone.*

VII.   *6th Tone.*

O . .   All ye . . bless ye the Lord :

VIII.   *7th Tone.*

O . . . . . .   All ye . . bless ye the Lord :

BENEDICITE, OMNIA OPERA.

O || ALL ye Works of the Lord, blefs ye the | Lord : praife Him, and magnify | Him for ev-er.

2 O ye Angels of the Lord, blefs ye the | Lord : praife Him, and magnify | Him for ev-er.

3 O ye Heavens, blefs ye the | Lord : praife Him, and magnify | Him for ev-er.

4 O ye Waters that be above the Firmament, blefs ye the | Lord : praife Him, and magnify | Him for ev-er.

5 O all ye Powers of the Lord, blefs ye the | Lord : praife Him, and magnify | Him for ev-er.

6 O ye Sun, and Moon, blefs ye the | LORD : praife Him, and magnify | Him for ev-er.

7 O ye Stars of Heaven, blefs ye the | LORD : praife Him, and magnify | Him for ev-er.

8 O ye Showers, and Dew, blefs ye the | LORD : praife Him, and magnify | Him for ev-er.

9 O ye Winds of GOD, blefs ye the | LORD : praife Him, and magnify | Him for ev-er.

10 O ye Fire and Heat, blefs ye the | LORD : praife Him, and magnify | Him for ev-er.

11 O ye Winter and Summer, blefs ye the | LORD : praife Him, and magnify | Him for ev-er.

12 O ye Dews, and Frofts, blefs ye the | LORD : praife Him, and magnify | Him for ev-er.

13 O ye Froft and Cold, blefs ye the | LORD : praife Him, and magnify | Him for ev-er.

14 O ye Ice and Snow, blefs ye. the | LORD : praife Him, and magnify | Him for ev-er.

15 O ye Nights, and Days, blefs ye the | LORD : praife Him, and magnify | Him for ev-er.

16 O ye Light and Darknefs, blefs ye the | LORD : praife Him, and magnify | Him for ev-er.

17 O ye Lightnings, and Clouds, blefs ye the | LORD : praife Him, and magnify | Him for ev-er.

18 O let the Earth blefs the | LORD : yea, let it praife Him, and magnify | Him for ev-er.

19 O ye Mountains, and Hills, blefs ye the LORD : praife Him, and magnify | Him for ev-er.

20 O all ye Green Things upon the Earth, blefs ye the | LORD : praife Him, and magnify | Him for ev-er.

21 O ye Wells, blefs ye the | LORD : praife Him, and magnify | Him for ev-er.

22 O ye Seas, and Floods, blefs ye the | LORD : praife Him, and magnify | Him for ev-er.

23 O ye Whales, and all that move in the Waters, blefs ye the | LORD : praife Him, and magnify | Him for ev-er.

24 O all ye Fowls of the Air, blefs ye the | LORD : praife Him, and magnify | Him for ev-er.

25 O all ye Beafts, and Cattle, blefs ye the | LORD : praife Him, and magnify | Him for ev-er.

26 O ye Children of Men, blefs ye the | LORD : praife Him, and magnify | Him for ev-er.

27 O let Ifrael blefs the | LORD : praife Him, and magnify | Him for ev-er.

28 O ye Priefts of the LORD, blefs ye the | LORD : praife Him, and magnify | Him for ev-er.

29 O ye Servants of the LORD, blefs ye the | LORD : praife Him, and magnify | Him for ev-er.

30 O ye Spirits and Souls of the Righteous, blefs ye the | LORD : praife Him and magnify | Him for ev-er.

31 O ye holy and humble Men of Heart, blefs ye the | LORD : praife Him, and magnify | Him for ev-er.

32 O Ananias, Azarias, and Mifael, blefs ye the | LORD : praife Him, and magnify | Him for ev-er.

GLORY BE TO THE FATHER, AND TO THE | SON : AND TO THE | HO-LY *GHOST;*

AS IT WAS IN THE BEGINNING, IS NOW, AND EVER | SHALL BE : WORLD WITHOUT | *END.* A-MEN.

BENEDICTUS.

S. LUKE I. 68.

I.   *1st Tone.*

II.   *1st Tone.*

III.   *4th Tone.*

IV.   *7th Tone.*

V.   *7th Tone.*

BENEDICTUS.

S. LUKE I. 68.

BLESS-ED || be the LORD | GOD of If-rael : for He hath vifited, and re- | deem-ed His‿*peo*-ple ;

2 And *hath* || raifed up a mighty fal- | va-tion for us : in the houfe of His | fer-vant *Da*-vid ;

3 As *He* || fpake by the mouth of His | ho-ly Pro-phets : which have been | fince the world be-gan ;

4 *That* || we fhould be faved | from our èn-emies : and from the hands of | all that *hate* us ;

5 *To* per- || form the mercy promifed to our | *fore*-fa-thers : and to remember His | ho-ly Co-ve-nant ;

6 *To* per- || form the oath which He fware to our fore- | fa-ther A-braham : that | He would *give* us ;

7 *That* || we being delivered out of the | hand of‿our èn-emies : might | ferve Him with‿*out* fear ;

8 *In* | holinefs and righteouf- | nefs be-fore Him : all the | days of *our* life.

9 *And* || thou, Child, fhalt be called the Prophet | of the High-eft : for thou fhalt go before the face of the LORD | to pre-pare His ways ;

10 To *give* || knowledge of falvation | ùnto His peo-ple : for the re- | mif-fion of their fins,

11 *Through* the || tender mercy | of our GOD : whereby the Day-fpring from on | high hath vifit-ed us ;

12 To *give* || light to them that fit in darknefs, and in the | fhàdow of *death* : and to guide our feet | in-to the‿way of peace.

GLO- || -RY BE TO THE FATHER, | AND TO THE‿SON : AND | TO THE HO-LY GHOST ;

AS *IT* || WAS IN THE BEGINNING, IS NOW, AND | EV-ER SHALL BE : WORLD WITHOUT | *END.* *A*-MEN.

BENEDICTUS.

S. LUKE I. 68.

BENEDICTUS.

S. LUKE I. 68.

B LESS-ED || be the Lord | God of Iſ-rael : for He
   hath viſited, | and re-deem-ed⌢His peo-ple ;

2 And *hath* || raiſed up a mighty ſal- | va-tion for us :
in the | houſe of⌢His ſer-vant Da-vid ;

3 As *He* || ſpake by the mouth of His | Ho-ly Pro-
phets : which have been | ſince the world be-*gan* ;

4 *That* || we ſhould be ſaved | from our èn-emies :
and from the | hands of all that hate us ;

5 *To* per- || form the mercy promiſed to our | *fore*-fa-
thers : and to re-˙| mem-ber⌢His ho-ly Cò-venant ;

6 *To* per- || form the oath which He ſware to our fore-|
fa-ther A-braham : that | *He would* give us ;

7 *That* || we being delivered out of the | hand of⌢our
èn-emies : might | ſerve ·Him with⌐*out* fear ;

8 *In* || holineſs and righteouſ- | neſs be-fore Him : all
the | days of *our life.*

9 *And* || thou, Child, ſhalt be called the Prophet | of
the High-eſt : for thou ſhalt go before the face of the |
Lord to pre⌐pare His *ways;*

10 To *give* || knowledge of ſalvation | ùnto His peo-
ple : for the re- | miſ-ſion of their *ſins,*

11 *Through* the || tender mercy | of our ·God :
whereby the Day-ſpring from on | high hath viſit-ed *us;*

12 To *give* || light to them that ſit in darkneſs, and in
the | ſhàdow of *death* : and to guide our feet | ìnto the
way of *peace.*

Glo- || -ry be to the Father | and to the⌢Son :
and | to the Ho-ly Ghost;

As *it* || was in the beginning, is now, and | ev-er
shall be : world with- | out end. *A-men.*

JUBILATE DEO.

PSALM C.

JUBILATE DEO.

PSALM C.

O BE ‖ joyful in the LORD, | all ye lands : ferve the LORD with gladnefs, and come before His | pre-fence with a⌒fong.

2 Be ye fure that the LORD | He is GOD : it is He that hath made us, and not we ourfelves; we are His people, and the | fheep of⌒His paf-ture.

3 O go your way into His gates with thankfgiving, and into His | courts with praife : be thankful unto Him, and fpeak | good of⌒His *Name.*

4 For the LORD is gracious, His mercy is | ev-er-laft-ing : and His truth endureth from generation to | ge-ne-ra-tion.

GLORY BE TO THE FATHER, | AND TO THE⌒SON : AND TO THE | HO-LY *GHOST;*

AS IT WAS IN THE BEGINNING, IS NOW, AND | EV-ER SHALL BE : WORLD WITHOUT | *END.* A-MEN.

Creed of S. Athanasius.

¶ Upon thefe Feafts ; *Chriftmas-Day*, the *Epiphany*, Saint *Matthias*, *Eafter-Day*, *Afcenfion-Day*, *Whit-Sunday*, Saint *John Baptift*, Saint *James*, Saint *Bartholomew*, Saint *Matthew*, Saint *Simon* and Saint *Jude*, Saint *Andrew*, and upon *Trinity-Sunday*, fhall be fung or faid at Morning Prayer, inftead of the Apoftles' Creed, this Confeffion of our Chriftian Faith, commonly called The Creed of Saint *Athanafius*, by the Minifter and people ftanding.

QUICUNQUE VULT.

8th Tone.

W HO-SO- || EVER will be fa-ved : before all things it is neceffary that he hold the | Càth-olick⁀ Faith.

2 Which Faith except every one do keep whole and unde- | fi-led : without doubt he fhall perifh ever- | làft-ingly.

3 And the Catholick Faith is | this : That we worfhip one GOD in Trinity, and Trinity in | Ù-nity ;

4 Neither confounding the | Per-fons : nor dividing the | Sub-ftance.

5 For there is one Perfon of the FATHER, another of the | SON : and another of the | Hò-ly⁀GHOST.

6 But the Godhead of the FATHER, of the SON, and of the HOLY GHOST, is all | one : the Glory equal, the Majefty co-e- | ter-nal.

7. Such as the FATHER is, fuch is the | SON : and fuch is the | Hò-ly⁀GHOST.

8 The FATHER uncreate, the SON uncre- | ate : and the HOLY GHOST | ùn-create.

9 The FATHER incomprehenfible, the SON incompre- |
hèn-fible : and the HOLY GHOST incrompre- | hèn-fible.

10 The FATHER eternal, the SON e- | ter-nal : and the
HOLY GHOST e- | ter-nal.

11 And yet They are not three e- | ter-nals : but one
e- | ter-nal.

12 As alfo there are not three incomprehenfibles,
nor three uncre- | a-ted : but one uncreated, and one
incompre- | hèn-fible.

13 So likewife the FATHER is Almighty, the SON
Al- | migh-ty : and the HOLY GHOST Al- | migh-ty.

14 And yet They are not three Al- | migh-ties : but
one Al- | migh-ty.

15 So the FATHER is GOD, the SON is | GOD : and the
HOLY GHOST | is GOD.

16 And yet They are not | three GODS : but | one
GOD.

17 So likewife the FATHER is LORD, the SON | LORD :
and the HOLY | GHOST LORD.

18 And yet not | three LORDS : but | one LORD.

19 For like as we are compelled by the Chriftian |
vè-rity : to acknowledge every Perfon by Himfelf to be
GOD | and LORD ;

20 So are we forbidden by the Catholick Re- | li-gion :
to fay, There be three GODS, or | three LORDS.

21 The FATHER is made of | none : neither created,
nor be- | got-ten.

22 The SON is of the FATHER a- | lone : not made,
nor created, but be- | got-ten.

23 The HOLY GHOST is of the FATHER, and of the |
SON : neither made, nor created, nor begotten, but
pro- | ceed-ing.

24 So there is one FATHER, not three FATHERS ; one

8th Tone.

Son, not | three Sons : one Holy Ghost, not three |
Hò-ly⁀Ghosts.

25 And in this Trinity none is afore, or after | o-ther :
none is greater, or lefs than a- | no-ther ;

26 But the whole three Perſons are co-eternal to- |
ge-ther : and co- | e-qual.

27 So that in all things, as is a- | fore-ſaid : the Unity
in Trinity, and the Trinity in Unity is to be | wòr-
ſhipped.

28 He therefore that will be | ſa-ved : muſt thus think
of the | Trì-nity.

1st Tone.

29 Furthermore, it is neceſſary to everlaſting ſal- |
vation : that he alſo believe rightly the Incarnation of
our Lord | Jè-sus⁀Christ.

30 For the right Faith is, that we believe and con- |
feſs : that our Lord Jesus Christ, the Son of God,
is | Gòd and⁀Man ;

31 God, of the Subſtance of the Father, begotten
before the | worlds : and Man, of the Subſtance of His .
Mother, born | ìn the⁀world ;

32 Perfect God, and perfect | Man : of a reaſonable
ſoul and human fleſh ſub- | ſiſt-ing ;

33 Equal to the FATHER, as touching His | Godhead : and inferior to the FATHER, as touching His | Man-hood.

34 Who although He be GOD and | Man : yet He is not two, but | one CHRIST ;

35 One ; not by converſion of the Godhead into | fleſh ; but by taking of the Manhood | in-to⌢GOD ;

36 One altogether ; not by confuſion of | Subſtance : but by unity of | Per-ſon.

37 For as the reaſonable ſoul and fleſh is | one man : ſo GOD and Man is | one CHRIST ;

38 Who ſuffered for our ſal- | vation : deſcended into hell, roſe again the third day | fròm the⌢dead.

39 He aſcended into Heaven, He ſitteth on the right hand of the FATHER, GOD Al- | mighty : from whence He ſhall come to judge the quick | ànd the⌢dead.

40 At Whoſe coming all men ſhall riſe again with their | bodies : and ſhall give account for | thèir own⌢ works.

41 And they that have done good ſhall go into life ever- | laſting : and they that have done evil into ever- | laſt-ing⌢fire.

8th Tone.

42 This is the Catholick | Faith : which except a man believe faithfully, he cannot be | ſa-ved.

GLORY BE TO THE FATHER, AND TO THE | SON : AND TO THE | Hò-ly⌢GHOST ;

AS IT WAS IN THE BEGINNING, IS NOW, AND EVER | SHALL BE : WORLD WITHOUT END. | A-MEN.

MAGNIFICAT.

S. LUKE I.

I. *5th Tone.*

II. *8th Tone.*

III. *3rd Tone.*

IV. *Irregular.*

V. *7th Tone.*

At Evening Prayer.

MAGNIFICAT.

S. LUKE I.

M Y ‖ foul doth magni- | fy the *Lord* : and my fpirit
hath rejoiced in | God my Sa-viour.

2 *For* ‖ He | hath re-gard-ed : the lowlinefs of | His
hand-maid-en.

3 For be- ‖ hold from | *hence-forth* : all generations
fhall | call me bleff-ed.

4 *For* ‖ He that is mighty hath | mag-ni-fi-ed⌢me :
and holy | is His *Name.*

5 And His ‖ mercy is on | them that fear Him :
throughout all | ge-ne-ra-tions.

6 He hath ‖ fhewed ftrength | with His *arm* : He hath
fcattered the proud in the imagination | of their *hearts.*

7 He hath ‖ put⌢down the mighty | from their *feat* :
and hath exalted the | hùmble and *meek.*

8 He hath ‖ filled the hungry | with good *things* : and
the rich he hath fent | emp-ty a⌢*way.*

9 He re- ‖ membering His mercy hath holpen His |
fer-vant Îf-rael : as He promifed to our forefathers,
Abraham and his | feed, for ev-er.

G*LO-*‖- RY BE TO THE F*ATHER,* | AND TO THE⌢S*ON* : AND
TO THE | HO-LY G*HOST;*

As it ‖ WAS IN THE BEGINNING, IS NOW, AND | EV-ER
SHALL BE : WORLD WITHOUT | END. A-*MEN.*

MAGNIFICAT.

S. LUKE I.

XI.   *4th Tone.*

MAGNIFICAT.

S. LUKE I.

MY || foul doth magni- | fy the LORD : and my fpirit hath rejoiced in | GOD my SA-VIOUR.

2 *For* || He | hath re-gard-ed : the lowlinefs of | His hand-*maid*-en.

3 For be- || hold, from | *hence-forth* : all generations fhall | call me *blef*-ed.

4 *For* || He that is mighty hath | mag-ni-fi-ed⌢me : and | ho-ly is His Name.

5 And His || mercy is on | them that fear Him : throughout all | ge-ne-*ra*-tions.

6 He hath || fhewed ftrength | with His *arm* : He hath fcattered the proud in the imagi- | na-tion of their hearts.

7 He hath || put⌢down the mighty | from their *feat* : and hath exalted the | hum-ble *and* meek.

8 He hath || filled the hungry | with good *things* : and the rich He hath | *fent* emp-ty away.

9 He re- || membering His mercy hath holpen His | fer-vant If-rael : as He promifed to our forefathers, Abraham and his | feed, for *ev*-er.

GLO-||-RY BE TO THE FATHER, | AND TO THE⌢SON : AND | TO THE HO-LY GHOST ;

AS IT || WAS IN THE BEGINNING, IS NOW, AND | EV-ER SHALL BE : WORLD WITHOUT | *END*. *A*-MEN.

MAGNIFICAT.

S. LUKE I.

XII.

M Y || foul doth magnify the | LORD : and my fpirit hath re- | jòiced in GOD my SA-VIOUR.

2 *For* || He hath re- | gard-ed : the lowlinefs of | *His* *hand*-maid-en

3 For be- || hold, from | hence-forth : all generations fhall | *call me* blef-fed.

4 *For* || He that is mighty hath magnified | me : and | ho-ly is His *Name.*

5 And His || mercy is on them that | fear Him : through- | out all ge-ne-ra-tions.

6 He hath || fhewed ftrength with His | arm : He hath fcattered the proud in the imagi- | na-tion of their *hearts.*

7 He hath || put¯down the mighty from their | feat : and hath exalted the | *hum*-ble and *meek.*

8 He hath || filled the hungry with good | things : and the rich He hath fent | *emp*-ty a-*way.*

9 He re- || membering His mercy hath holpen His fervant Ifra- | el : as He promifed to our forefathers Abraham | and his feed, for ev-er.

GLO- || -RY BE TO THE FATHER, AND TO THE | SON : AND | TO THE HO-LY *GHOST;*

As IT || WAS IN THE BEGINNING, IS NOW, AND EVER | SHALL BE : WORLD WITHOUT | *END. A-MEN.*

MAGNIFICAT. (Service Form.)

S. LUKE I.

My ſoul doth mag-ni-fy the Lord : and my ſpirit hath re-joic-ed in God .. my Saviour. For He hath re-gard-ed : the low-li-neſs of His hand-maid-en. For behold, from henceforth : all generations ſhall call me bleſſ-ed. For He that is migh-ty hath mag-ni-fi-ed me : and ho-ly is ... His Name.

And His mer - cy is on them that fear Him : throughout

all ge-ne - ra - tions. He hath ſhew-ed ſtrength with His arm :

He hath ſcattered the proud in the imagi - na - tion of their hearts.

He hath put down the migh - ty from their ſeat : and

hath ex - alt - ed the hum - ble and meek. He . . hath

fill - ed the hun - gry with good things : and the rich He hath

sent emp - ty .. a - way. He ... re - mem-bering His

mer - cy hath hol - pen His fer - vant If - - ra - el :

as He promifed to our forefathers, Abraham and his feed, for ev - er.

Glo - ry be to the FA - THER, and to the SON : and

to the Ho - ly Ghost; As it was in the be-gin-ning, is

now, and ev-er shall be : world without end. A - - - men.

MAGNIFICAT.   (Service Form.)

S. LUKE I.

Andante Divoto. Full.   *In 1st mode.*

My foul . . doth mag-ni-fy the Lord : and my spirit hath re -

- joic - ed in God my Sa - viour. For He hath re-gard-ed : the low - li - nefs of His hand-maid-en. For behold, from henceforth ·

all ge-ne - ra - tions fhall call me blefs - ed. For He that is

migh-ty hath mag - ni - fi - ed me : and ho - ly is . . His Name.

And His mer - cy is on them that fear Him : thro'-out all

ge - ne - ra - tions. He hath fhew - ed ftrength with His arm :

He hath fcattered the proud in the imagi- na-tion of their hearts.

He hath put down the migh - ty from their feat :

and hath ex - alt - ed the hum - - ble and meek.

He hath fill - ed the hun - gry with good things :

and the rich He hath fent emp - ty a - way. He re -

- membering His mercy hath holp-en His fer-vant If - ra - el :

as He promifed to our forefathers, A-bra-ham and his feed for ev - er.

Glo - ry be to the FA - THER, and to the Son : and

to the Ho - ly Ghost; As it was in the beginning, is now, and

ev - er fhall be : world with - out end. A - - men.

NUNC DIMITTIS.

S. LUKE II. 29.

I.   5th Tone.

II.   7th Tone.

III.   Irregular.

IV.   5th Tone.

V.   1st Tone.

VI.   *3rd Tone.*

VII.   *6th Tone.*

NUNC DIMITTIS.

S. LUKE II. 29.

L ORD, || now letteſt Thou Thy ſervant de- | part in
peace : according | to Thy *word.*

2 *For* || mine | eyes have *ſeen* : Thy | . ſal-va-tion.

3 *Which* || Thou | haſt pre-par-ed : before the face
of | *all* peo-ple ;

4 To be || a‿light to | light-en the‿Gen-tiles : and to
be the glory of Thy | peo-ple Ìf-rael.

GLO- || -RY BE TO THE FATHER, | AND TO THE‿*SON* :
AND TO THE | HO-LY *GHOST* ;

AS IT || WAS IN THE BEGINNING, IS NOW, AND | EV-ER
SHALL BE : WORLD WITHOUT | END. A-*MEN.*

✠

NUNC DIMITTIS. (Service Form.)

S. LUKE II. 29.

Lord, now lett-eſt Thou Thy ſer - vant de - part in peace :

ac-cord-ing to Thy word. For mine eyes have ſeen : Thy ſal-

- va - tion. Which Thou haſt pre - par - ed : before the face of

all peo - ple. To be a light to light-en the Gen-tiles :

and to be the glory of Thy peo - ple If - - ra - - el.

Glo-ry be to the FA-THER, and to the SON : and to the

Ho - LY GHOST ; As it was in the be - gin - ning, is

now, and ev - er fhall be : world with-out end. A - men.

NUNC DIMITTIS. (SERVICE FORM.)

S. LUKE II. 29.

Moderato. Full.   In 7th mode.

LORD, now letteft Thou Thy fer - vant de - part in peace : ac -

- cord-ing to Thy word. For mine eyes have feen : Thy fal - va - tion.

Which Thou haſt pre - par - ed : be - fore the. face of all peo-ple ;

To be a light to light - en the Gen - tiles : and to be the glory of Thy

peo-ple Iſ - - ra - el. Glory be to the FA-THER, and to the SON :

and to the HO-LY GHOST ; As it was in the beginning, is now, and

ev - er ſhall be : world with - out end. A - - men.

London : Henderson, Rait, and Fenton, General Printers, 23 Berners Street, Oxford Street, W.

.